THERE IS NEWS ALONG THE OHIO RIVER

PLAINWATER NONFICTION SERIES

THERE IS NEWS ALONG THE OHIO RIVER

BETH GILSTRAP

Published in the United States of America

Library of Congress Cataloging-in-Publication Data
Gilstrap, Beth, 1977–
There Is News Along the Ohio River / Beth Gilstrap.
ISBN-13: 979-8-9926116-5-6
Subjects: LCSH: Memoir, Nature, Southern Literature.
LCGFT: Nonfiction.

Library of Congress Control Number: 2025942182

Cover and interior design by Alban Fischer
Cover and title page photos by Beth Gilstrap

RIVER RIVER BOOKS
10 Linganore Place
Durham, NC 27707

www.riverriverbooks.org

For the bridge walkers

I learned how to make a honey reduction of the ugly sentences.
Still, my voice cracks.

—TERESE MARIE MAILHOT

I.

There is news along the Ohio River: you have moved five hundred miles from the only home you've ever known. The sky feels bigger here but that's the lack of canopy, the way the land is bisected by her, how the bridges span rusted bright, shadows on the current. Have you ever stood leaning over a hot railing not caring much if you fell while watching a great blue heron dip and glide, swoop and flap into the wide open past the Slugger Museum, thinking about the false notion of time and how the bat your elder sibling kept close when your father was expected held the same burned-in brand? The wings, the wings, they feel like lonesome so high up, but a lonesome on the cusp of release.

II.

There is news along the Ohio River: two sour cherries lollygag on the Indiana side whispering tales of buckets and coughing out reminiscences of hard work, how it feels to split two joined at the stem and drop one into a lover's open palm; they say you'll remember one day, one day you'll bite down, release tart sugars that catch in your jaw, and break into a smile like nobody's business.

III.

There is news along the Ohio River: a woman has planted fuschia coneflower in the four by six patch of earth outside a hundred-year-old home she's borrowing for now. She has no idea if the separation will stick, if he'll stay sober, if she'll ever raise enough tomatoes in pots or native flowers to unmeek her heart, to unsee her traumas, or at least lay them to rest and let the roots do their root magic. In the geraniums she's hung in yellow pots all along the back fence, s-hooks remind her of a boy named Reed and the chain which did him in but the annuals themselves are Italian nonnas going about their business hoisting ceramic water pitchers, beating out fine, fine rugs which show their age, but they like patina, they like lemons and butter, fingers threaded with dough. There's not a gaunt one among them, not like the lady next door who takes care of her bedridden matriarch, grandkids who say they prefer foster care *'cause at least they could eat what they want there*, and an elder brother who wears goggles to walk his baby dolls up the street every day in a stroller. Her faded heart tattoo is still a heart despite its condition, threshed by circumstance and during those active summer months she mows her yard patch on Friday evenings just in case someone comes, just in case someone comes to help.

IV.

There is news along the Ohio River: a porcelain-haired woman has planted herself on a bench in Indiana, her gaze on Kentucky. People escaping slavery crossed this river on their way to Ohio and freedom. There is a marker for Hannah Toliver on which they still use the word *fugitive* and you think *connotation matters, word choice matters,* you wield them after all. Fuck the writer of that sign, probably put up by a white person with good intentions, but the river won't ask this woman holding the bench's arm why she thinks she might float away any second. The river will just keep on shifting color and shape and when she recedes, marks, demarcation lines. Before and after and the land beyond return. For the first time in your life, as she closes her eyes and turns her cheekbones upward to the sun, you long for ancient times when it would have been nothing and everything to remove her shoes and wash her feet.

v.

There is news along the Ohio River: a man in mud-bottomed jeans has propped himself up on his backpack, knees bent, eating vegetarian baked beans from a single serving can. You think of the hundreds of times you've eaten them, stirred thick with chipotle pepper and smoked salt, aged cheddar charred on top. You know you need protein. Beans are easy and you need to remember to order can openers by the dozen and drop them in the free pantry. It hasn't been so long since he's had a haircut; he looks like a boy you knew who died young. He looks like Patrick when you talked on a mountaintop in Harpers Ferry, when you talked about John Brown and the feeling of a fight coming but that was the nineties and you didn't know shit. He looks like Patrick, freckled and small-framed, a water-damaged paperback poking out of his bag. He looks like Patrick before you shared a joint on a dilapidated porch back home. He looks like Patrick before the shotgun.

VI.

There is news along the Ohio River: a woman in overalls has perched on a good rock high water has nudged a few feet from shore over months, over a year, on days and nights and wicked limbo, cloaked in mist howling before the breakbeat of sun, however brief in this midsouth sky. This is what dawn looks like here. She cups her hands, waiting while the wind catches wisps of hair adding to the mad look we get at a certain age when a quick glance says *fuck if I'll let it happen again*. You could join her. It would only take a skip and there would be solace in her crow's feet, in the billow of her scarf and the parchment she has rolled out before her knees, held down by two mugs, one steaming, one cold and clear, awaiting pigment, awaiting feathers, and maybe even gasoline.

VII.

There is news along the Ohio River: a recently separated woman makes a pot of minestrone for the friends who've brought her here. Homemade stock in cast iron almost too heavy to lift filled with corn cob and onion, garden sage and thyme, onion scraps and a whole head of garlic cut in half with a solid Japanese knife. She plays a Carole King record she's loved since girlhood and lets the steam gather on her face. How they picked her up off the floor more than once before she lost them. There is news along the Ohio and today, it's a beaver doing quiet work on a felled pine to pull her back to the business of living.

VIII.

There is news along the Ohio River: a ragweed thicket lilts, heavy from its own blooming. Unearthly, circumspect of the small humans jumping flat-footed in splash pools, playing that rusted xylophone on the playground built to look like a steamship—the Belle of Louisville—which 2020 docked for the longest period since its birth in the nineteenth century; if she could think, would she wonder what she's done wrong? There is spirit in objects if only you'd look for it. Think on the laws of physics. Place a hand on two-hundred-year-old rails and feel the hands of your ancestors, ungloved, turn numb. But the ragweed wonders, too. Whether the children will rip their flowers for crowns. There is some merit there, in the wisps of kid hair, rendered victorious, emblems not of autonomy, nor vagrancy, but of yearning, yearning the way hardtack yearns for butter, for powdered sugar, for sweet lips.

IX.

There is news along the Ohio River: the town of Jeffersonville has installed a baby box and a Narcan vending machine near the bridge. It's nestled there amid the historic candy shop and the restaurant with red velvet pancakes she bought herself on mother's day. She wonders if she'll go to prison if she winds up using both. There's been a terrible drought of support since coming down from the mountains back east. At least then, folks would stop by with diapers and a casserole from time-to-time. She'd pick at the crunchy canned onions while doing what she called the baby dance, which was something like a step, ball, change from her early years. She couldn't help but think of crinoline and her grandmama's powder puff, housed in gold and smelling rich. It's good to know it's there, the box. She has a Narcan kit the doctor gave her when her blood came back marked with something didn't nobody prescribe her. Docs back home didn't ask for stories. She always wondered who was supposed to revive her if she was unconscious until the day she dropped the last of her change in the jukebox at the dive bar, sweating sick and pounding beers until they took the edge off for the last time.

X.

There is news along the Ohio River: these are extraordinary days here when the late summer light shifts Faulknerian and monarchs alight on the spans of the Big Four Bridge. The woman likes to think they help the drowned men from the 1897 disaster rise up from the depths just to catch a glimpse of the work they did still standing, but now instead of steam trains carrying passengers and coal to Chicago and St. Louis, she comes to toss rose petals in the water while a man drops pistachio shells behind him every day like he's trying to find his way home to a place that no longer exists. At the full moon, witches draw circles, light candles, incense, and leave offerings, defiant and unafraid. And the children puff up their chests with bravery to let their mamas hold them high so they can wave at the barges headed north. Amid all this wonder, this awe she can't touch, a butterfly is clipped by a pigeon, how it falls reminds her of a married photographer who once told her on the road to St. Augustine how he hated to see them on the highway. *It tears me up—the resemblance to falling angels when they get hit*. She follows its descent and float. After it's no longer visible, she looks at her feet. The right shoe has begun opening up from the miles and she keeps on wondering about the photographer, sacred insects, how time usually plods along, exalted in its season, but sometimes a crane breaks and time swallows.

XI.

There is news along the Ohio River: some days she has no idea why she moved here to live alone in a house built when her Mee-maw was still sweeping the speck of yard out front of mill housing. It's angry, the house. The shower floods the kitchen. Slugs come through outlets to mate on the walls and the mess of it is revelation. The voice of ancestors saying, *no, love, no*. This is no more permanent than the longing for fog, for underworld, for touch.

XII.

There is news along the Ohio River: a boy, toddler drunk, walks ahead of his parents whose body language suggests distance, a slow dying of affection, skin hunger. See how she reaches for his hand and he doesn't register—they call that a bid, a turn toward, but to those who know better, a lament. See how they fail to notice the child following a faint blood trail looping its way up the bridge, trying to find its source but failing to connect it to the smallest of feathers, some hovering in their footfalls.

XIII.

There is news along the Ohio River: he comes to visit and asks about her anger, how it's doing, like her shadow's learned to breathe. She tells him it's still there but maybe not quite as bad with some distance, wonders if he has any idea how difficult it was to keep him alive. She shows him the Big Four, buys them cappuccinos from a shop that hosts Dungeons & Dragons tournaments. She used to be the master sometimes, she confesses, but not on the real game, on the version she and her elder sibling played out in the yard when their mama was at work and they looked after each other on sick days, teacher work days, most of summer. She has never recovered from that period, not really, and the old anger mixed with the new has driven her to drink, walk, weep, on repeat like some tragic Victorian protagonist not yet sure she can untangle it all. He misses her more when he's packing his things. She shimmies and sings to seventies rock in the kitchen where the dogs join in with their dinosaurs and the pot's about to boil over. She sends her husband postcards, still trying to add brightness to his fractured days. She does not tell him about the divers who go deep into the river or how they recently found tennis shoes tied to a cinder-block a few feet off shore.

XIV.

There is news along the Ohio River: a man in orange sneakers walks the bridge nearly every day—alone, same as you. He gives a wave like a father saying farewell to a child he's taught to drive, a hand coarse with work on the line at Ford all those years. Ridges and impressions in thin but neat nails. On days he's not there, you worry. Accidents. Trauma. Old injuries climbing their way up and needling those bundles of nerves from low back and down into thigh meat, where the hair isn't as full as it used to be, but his aviators gleam and he points to the hawk, to the great blue heron, to the red-winged blackbirds' chipper return, always making sure you see though you never share a word.

XV.

There is news along the Ohio River: a man has opened all the windows in his century home with its bronze plaque and mouth-blown windows. His snow-faced dog rests on a pillow on the first floor while the man plays a mournful song on French horn and even from a distance, she can see the way his back crooks and feel the ache traipse into the small of hers, the pressure, the pressure, to keep on playing when the ginkgo leaves have all dropped at once and the house is empty again. And wonder, wonder asks if he can smell the river up there as he spins once before the gods send him a light percussion on the metal roof in the form of raindrops and the patter of squirrels.

XVI.

There is news along the Ohio River: an owl pellet inch rolls past dandelions blooming in cracks in the sidewalk. A heart juxtaposed. Human versus *tyto alba*. Barn Owl. You dissect without fear for this time what's died is for a reason, and likely unborn for the beaks are so small they remind you of the interior doves of sand dollars you sometimes broke open while yet they lived—pinkish green, supple with hair that tried to grab onto your palm, to sink back down beneath the sand. You cannot help but cry at the enormity of it all, the slight you feel as you count two, four, six, and ribs by the dozen, held in thumbnail and happenstance.

XVII.

There is news along the Ohio River: a woman wishes she knew how to play fiddle as she catches sight of her left foot again. It still turns in when she's anxious. A tiger orange shoe against a red bar, the synchronicity of being called Tin Man in her high school circle, how folks made fun of her mental illness because she was too sick to pass for normal, as though her father's hand had left permanent marks on her sore shin bone where he whacked her every time her foot went its own way.

XVIII.

There is news along the Ohio River: it is the end of what people on the news will eventually call the *George Floyd Summer* and someone has spray painted *Where is the love?* on the Indiana side of the Big Four in black and red. The "w" curls wide and tight and there's an arrow connecting the words. She feels it in the pocket between rib and collarbone where so much trauma lives. Radiant heat. How he helped by hanging better, light-filtering shades in the front room, but the sparrows keep getting in through gaps, through breaks, through rot, and she can't seem to find an answer even with meds, even sober, even in quiet funerals for birds.

XIX.

There is news along the Ohio River: a woman thinks of her great grandmother who taught her and her friend to play double dutch—there's something on the breeze that reads *jump rope*. She was over ninety and her hands, thin skin injured just from the momentum of swinging, all the while her apron bouncing one, two, one, two, hop, jump, clap, squeal until one of us trips but it's never her even with her arm in a cast and snuff in her pocket.

xx.

There is news along the Ohio River: a man has hopped off his bike to follow her. She begins to jog despite that flexor tear that's never healed right but he cuts off her path. It is broad day. *Whatever that means*, she thinks. Broad. Safety isn't guaranteed by where earth is in its turning, god knows she's learned that, if nothing else. Graves and gavels and gall. He tells her he's in the FBI. Tells her he's military. Tells her all his buddies were killed in Afghanistan. Asks to walk with her, just a walk, just a walk, he says. After weaving away, creating distance, required, needed, distance. He says he's wealthy. Insurance settlements. Disability. FBI. Comments on her walking tights, brand new, swirled to look like nebulae, and before she finally, finally speaks up, says you are scaring me. *Mercy. Mercy. Mercy*, she thinks of the Horsehead nebula, glowing red from hydrogen, how it takes fifteen-hundred years for its light to reach us and looks east, wondering about the night sky here in this new city so far from home.

XXI.

There is news along the Ohio River: a woman draped in white and gray could be built into the dock, her colors merge with fog into the din of longing and a ghost bridge waiting to bring along more spirits into the breach, the liminal swells of seagull and dove. Her feet dangle over the edge but her hands are pinched between her knees, a punishment, an isolation, a lip drunk on its own right to quiver, to crack chapped and into a different kind of gloaming where she thinks *I'm alone* like a metronome.

XXII.

There is news along the Ohio River: the bridge is papered with fliers for an activist reporter gone missing. Last seen at a nearby public pool where he was asked to leave for nonpayment. He's cut his locs since he wrote about voter suppression for *The Courier-Journal*, since writing about black fathers who have to teach their kids hypervigilance, since writing about the parents whose 14-year-old was held at gunpoint by LMPD even before Breonna's murder. Since interviewing another grieving mother, this time, of a beloved hometown barbecue man shot during the protests, for no reason. Gone missing. Imagine this child's trauma breaking loose, the child's heart beating when his mama asks for privacy as they get him some help. Gone missing. As if there's no cause for it. Gone missing. Since giving voice to the West End. Gone missing since writing *the greatest white privilege: life*. He is found safe this time and Lord, we should see all the timelines at once. The family asks for understanding, for grace. The pleading so evident, so ignored by white readers who supported him when he was doing that good palatable work, before the volta, before the last straw floats down into his own trembling hand.

XXIII.

There is news along the Ohio River: one of the ducks has been banished. He hobbles along to find a sunny spot facing east. Could she sidle up next to him? Could she scoop him up and carry him across the bridge to the place she's living? *Not home,* she thinks. *Powerless. You can't save everything* her husband said once. The woman wonders if anyone else cares, if anyone else sees, how to get her hands on tenderness so they might survive winter nestled around the space heater and twinkling silver lights.

XXIV.

There is news along the Ohio River: a juvenile robin has flown into the glass door at an abandoned restaurant, Louisville side. It has a little overhang, this entryway to thick dusted benches upturned, chained together. A woman walks past little darling, her heel-rubbing boots already opening up skin there at the beginning. The robin has puffed up, a trauma response, though the woman thinks nothing of it yet, just *little darling, little darling, come home with me* like no one else she knows, collecting, building a coterie of small things to care for, small things already lost, shadows of dander, fleas, and glory iridescent. It's the motion of her feet that matters, it keeps her exiled in translucent suffering, but unreachable as flocks intact, a murmuration turned saint, anointed in honey and olive oil, clary sage, and the blood of the fanged, a reaping-hook in the throat left behind, a monument to righteousness. Doesn't it collect like phlegm there behind the molars? In an hour, the wind has chapped her chin on this coldest day of the year, still weeks from the solstice, but the robin has not budged and so she sits with her darling, petting her crown, singing songs about mama's little baby loving shortening, shortening while they wait for wildlife rescue to scoop her up into a towel-lined shoebox where, in the dark, she might recover her senses.

XXV.

There is news along the Ohio River: it's two weeks shy of the solstice and the circus has come to fracture the expanding Kentuckiana gray. They have come—without animals blessed be—in repurposed school buses painted rosemary green. They have come in old ice cream trucks outfitted with solar panels. They have come in Muck boots and fleece with sledge hammers and showy muscles and butter-flavored oil. They have come to raise the tent against winter. They have come with tales of failure and oddity and the flourish of chosen family. They take turns hammering. The petite feminine one *yahs* so hard when they swing you swear we've all returned to particle, leaving these fallible bodies behind, but after a beat, after a breath, broad shoulders removes their pentacled hat, takes the hammer, and with a metal on metal shriek you are front row center watching them wriggle and wriggle until the straightjacket loosens, until their shoulders bloom like rhododendron and your broke down heart long since set to rest on cinderblocks, begins to hum and before you know it, there you are again, crying in a roomful of strangers.

XXVI.

There is news along the Ohio River: on Christmas Eve, the mist is freezing to the rails on the Big Four Bridge and a woman removes her shearling gloves to touch ice crystals forming in divots on the rusted iron; a man, eight-layer bundled, lights prayer candles around gifts he's pulled from his cart—deodorant, shampoo, wet wipes and warm socks, pen and ink drawings on thick paper, cheddar popcorn in twist-tied baggies, crayons and bottled water—when he blows the flame out on the incense stick he used to light them he bows his head, the smoke winding up around his shoulders before settling back into his puffed up torso, a shawl of holiness.

XXVII.

There is news along the Ohio River: in their doldrums, the geese have huddled facing east but there is no sun today. You have returned from North Carolina where you wiped sweat from your upper lip on Christmas Day feeling mutant in the place that forged you, having never mastered the art of crypsis, a kind of natural mimicry, but you can code switch like a motherfucker to stay a thin kind of safe. If only you could have concealed yourself to look like the branch on which you perch, you might have built a formidable home there but you are encased in a body feminine so home eludes you, an unfortified earthen hut during the wet season. *The goal is to divert the water*, he says, when you live in floodplains and isn't the whole world becoming. Becoming electrified in a hospital gown mis-tied, showing the deep unhealed torch cut from your liver but necessity is a mother and the garment will do just to get outside for a little while and bum a cigarette off a gunshot wound talking about senescence, *what a trip, baby girl, what a trip*.

XXVIII.

There is news along the Ohio River: you speak to mother for the first time in months. Early January and she warns of danger, tells you to stay off the streets. Stolen elections and scamdemics. To stock your nine hundred square feet with dry goods and water. Dry goods and ammunition though you have no gun. You rub your ragged jaw, your body keeping the score, holding neglect and rage there so much it has begun to crumble as you search for words to unknot the tangles from a mind you once respected.

XXIX.

There is news along the Ohio River: a woman crosses the Big Four today in *ice maiden* boots, dreaming of the break of pine trees in an ice storm back home, the way she can breathe in the same smell her people way back smelled when they had to hunt and skin and build fires for cast iron pots—she feels these women in the ache of her right hip, where repressed sadness goes to hide, a spot no one's kissed since the worm moon years ago. She slides in spite of thick rubber traction, but the bridge is open so she walks on. All of yesterday's footprints have formed memories, slick, ephemeral joy occasions, snow day occasions, in a path around a frozen field mouse whose pulse there's no use in checking, but since no one's looking, she leans down and speaks her sore heart.

xxx.

There is news along the Ohio River: a woman snaps photos of debris. January here is angry and wields its power like a scythe to the collarbone. A wheelchair lies on its back, a hospital name she doesn't recognize stamped on its seat. It is fully functional, if a little beat up. She recognizes its extra width, wants to be optimistic at the start of a new year, but she's seen too much for old nonsense. She wants to believe the chair's last occupant healed and pushed that motherfucker into the water herself, but she thinks of Connie, her jewelry for every holiday and season boxed up, tucked in the back of her nightstand where she won't have to see it.

XXXI.

There is news along the Ohio River: you've lost feeling in your pinky where the sharp fingernail has worn a hole through a glove meant for folks farther south than here, where sleeping outside ain't so bad sometimes when the fireflies come up in the woods off the overpass and you can tie a beat-up cage you found on the side of the road to a bottle full of brackish brown water and pull up blue crab. You hitched a ride to Kentucky last summer on a pig truck, parted ways with the man in Butchertown where he said, *Bubba, you're gonna need these up here,* but you wished he'd told you how they lock the public restrooms in winter. Even in bright dry day. Even when the water's up. Even when the shelter over in Jeffersonville is at capacity and you're too tired to try another downtown.

XXXII.

There is news along the Ohio River: rains and snowmelt to the east have brought the detritus of winter, intact evergreens, Mountain Dew bottles, a cormorant drying her wings atop a tire floating by at a good click like an old god on his way home to New Orleans. But it's the fridge that gets you, the fridge just like one Mee-Maw had out back of the house you used to play in when folks didn't much throw things away because they'd survived a depression in the south and had all them babies to feed and if something could be reused damn if they wouldn't find a way. Busted bathtubs grow damn fine tomatoes and sage she'd pick down to nubs, apron pockets bulging, to dry in open windows over late summer days. *Don't it smell good,* the old ones said. *One day you'll do the same.* But kids never think so when they're dreaming up babies and households that don't need herbal remedies. Fine silks and polished new everything. But babies were rampant in those days and they didn't have to fill out forms for exploratory tests, the babies, they just kept coming moonlike in cycles, swathed in handmade quilts, enwrapped in folklore, sadness always banging its way in the side, the crack of the screen door obliterating Mee-maw's nerves while she was washing black dye out of Aunt Joe's hair in the kitchen sink, and when she had her wet head knotted up good, she rose, bringing the cigarette she never put down to her lips and said, *well, look here if that grandbaby of yours ain't obliterated her dress.*

XXXIII.

There is news along the Ohio River: you have come to call her Mama, this water. Today she is high and rising still, ornery in the midday sun, carrying trees that stood tall and reaching for five of your lifetimes to their final destinations. The way Mama strips their bark, leaving them smooth and rolling, how they turn and you know it's not so far-fetched to wade in—you can hold your own in angry currents—to hug a log close and ride. You wonder what the water would feel like between your toes, the grit and gristle, buckeyes and cornstalks gathering more speed than you, light as they are. There are behemoth catfish down there lumbering along the bottom and in your exhale, piano, a memory scavenged from your genetic mother's hands somehow tapping the keys, somber and wailing as far downriver as anything.

XXXIV.

There is news along the Ohio River: a young man has tied his loosening jeans up with twine and huddles into his denim jacket, a bird peeking out of a nest, but the fabric may as well be a brittle photograph wet and dried a hundred times before he taped it over the crack in the rear window of the sedan where he dwells. He calls out to the gods for proficiency enough at survival but his prayers don't count, he knows, not when his dad's a good Christian who votes for good Christian men who walk around unconcealed, brown silt loam fertile and sanctimonious. His eyes look wet when he asks if you'd like some company, slurs *beautiful* and *body* into a rhythm like Sanskrit and the Empress card flashes an image of sherpa and steaming broth where his mama combs the mats from his hair but all you can muster is *that's sweet, love, but I'm married* and you are even if he lives five hundred miles south, even if he had the same mind-altered gait not so long ago, even if you want to tell them both things have a way, things have a way, we'll be okay, but you know how easily comfort slides from our hands.

XXXV.

There is news along the Ohio River: two siblings, one rainbow-socked with purple sunglasses and a head of returning hair are regulars, too. They're a walking monument to decades of tease and giggle. The shorter, the younger, the healthier of the two has the markings of distress and sometimes, you can see by the way she keeps one hand hovering at the other's back, how she tries to hold on.

XXXVI.

There is news along the Ohio River: you have not filled your pockets with rocks. You have not thought about how beautiful a view it would be if you jumped on a cloudless day, how you would meet your new mother with your toes pointed and arms wide because you never learned to dive as the Great Lakes gulls sound the alarm.

XXXII.

There is news along the Ohio River: a child has tied their mittens to the railing. Beneath the ice, bubbles. Movement, shift. Physics. Building to the great seasonal breaking loose and the observer kneels in gratitude of the sacrifice. Twists of cotton candy pink and blue, of the child's warmth, the hope of glitter polish shining in the sun.

XXXIII.

There is news along the Ohio River: the flood comes later this year and after, there are no signs of younglings. She begs herself not to think about Rachel Carson's silence, not to wrap her arms in every shred of fishing line she's gathered here on the banks. No one will understand the protest, why cutting off the blood flow is symbolic like amaranth—also known as love-lies-bleeding, also known as kiwicha, also known as *Amaranthus caudatus*—she planted out front of the sinking house with its murder sparrows. No one will understand the instinct to dive on a grenade when nobody asked you to. As she picks the crusted burnt skin on her wrist and thinks of Bourdain, she remembers the scars make you legit. But she's only out here on the bridge trying not to recognize how the tone of their friendship changed after she moved here. The word *support*. How careful she is not to pop her p's when she records talks about writing. Rooted in *portare*, Latin for *carry*. No matter how many cakes she's baked, no matter how fresh the berries, no matter how perfect the crumb or the way hot Crisco pools and turns the top of the cornbread that good kind of brown, none of it can make their love permanent. She knows she's cooking for ghosts.

XXXIX.

There is news along the Ohio River: you have walked these banks, this bridge, this borderland of metal, earth, and water for eighteen months. You have added to your dead. Starlings. Geese. A goat after the tornadoes raged through western Kentucky. A doe, whose soft ear danced in a circle and you fell to your knees for all you couldn't save. Your father-in-law whose spirit reached you on the bridge itself in an image of bare feet in a door way, a border collie guarding his body.

XL.

There is news along the Ohio River: pink buds have thrown their magic at her once again—a magic she must touch, fingertips of restraint making her mind wander to the tulip poplar and the prickly pear cactus planted in the hull of a great willow oak felled before she was born, how the spines pierced her toddler palms, the bloodletting into mycelium and the opuntia where it can take four years to fruit. She does not yet know the pinks are edible. She breaks them open to paint her white shoes, the broken sidewalk, her own cheeks before instinctively returning its desiccated remains to the earth, a good spot near the center where she's not supposed to climb, where she remembers her knees are not ladylike enough for a dress.

XLI.

There is news along the Ohio River: you carry a baby bunny's remains across the bridge to Kentucky. This kind of death few others would notice happens so often now you barely react until the burial is over, until you've found a sunny spot next to the red-veined sorrel, until you have wrapped the infant in gold-tinged tissue paper, until you have gently scooped the river rich earth on top, until you have patted it down, still careful not to break its tiny bones, until you've picked a shirttail of wild violets and dandelion, until you've said you're sorry this happened, go in peace. It's not until you throw your bloodwet jacket in the washer and scrub your hands with lavender soap and a hard-bristle brush you remember the golden retriever, the horror of his human, the school children at their back, how you announced, *it's okay, it'll be alright, I have him.*

XLII.

There is news along the Ohio River: red tulips have risen, lemon balm is greening, reaching, getting ready for the bees, pollen gathered like yellow pompoms on thin little legs known formally as *corbicula*, or pollen baskets for the optimists. Bees have a heart that runs from the brain, through the thorax and down the back of the abdomen. Imagine the weight.

XLIII.

There is news along the Ohio River: a woman reads at the feet of bronze Abraham Lincoln and his books on law and the Bible. Does she wonder if Lincoln ever read the drumbeat abolitionist words of Maria Stewart? How she called for equality in education for black women long before slavery was abolished. How she spoke in public. Her audacity. Does she wonder if he ever read Phillis Wheatley's elegies and hymns? Wollstonecraft's manifesto? Sit with a pipe and mull over Shelly's comments on the grotesque, the monstrous? Does this beauty who has kicked off her sandals savor the inhale of solitude cradled there in big mythology of this image of a man or is she there for the dragonflies dancing above that well-placed stovepipe hat and the radiant heat loosening the muscles in her tired feet?

XLIV.

There is news along the Ohio River: a man has washed his clothes with bar soap and draped them over the wall to dry while he charges his phone at the docks and another unfolds a mesh chair, opens a cup of chicken livers to warm in the thin March sun to get good and stinky just like your grandfather had all those years ago when he hoisted you on his shoulders where you saw the Ferris wheel spinning along down the shore like it was weighed down with mud and in its labored mechanics, your future, your hands reaching for river water like it gave birth to you.

XLV.

There is news along the Ohio River: the knockout roses have begun their business of sweeting the air but the backbeat of melt, of rot, is always there. Mama is cleansing herself, her babies, and sending all that gunk—forest floor, dip cans, even Captain America's shield—down and out. What will we make of such artifacts while fish are dwindling and those left rise to the surface to get a quick look at animals draped in the hubris of dominion, and find a father teaching a child to run a hook through a caterpillar who could have been a monarch?

XLVI.

There is news along the Ohio River: the town of Jeffersonville is floating a stage downriver from storage. It is late spring after snowmelt has done its duty of pushing the unearthed, the discarded, the discontent, roaring, trickling out and through. They say it's the only way, the Jungians, the coaches, the spin cyclists hopping up and out of the saddle, pushing until we all tear apart. Love will come again but this timeline, it won't come in wombs nor whispers at jawlines, not in nursing, not the kind at your breast anyway, but in the fine mist gathering on the chins of onlookers, in the offbeat claps of strangers howling at a Stevie Nicks cover sung by a woman with coins sewn into her skirt, in the accents of ghosts, dragging her heart around.

XLVII.

There is news along the Ohio River: a woman walks the bridge because she doesn't know what else to do. She has not talked to her father-in-law much since she left North Carolina. As she removes her hoodie and ties it around her waist, she thinks of the ugly on purpose tie she gave him that first Christmas at their apartment, and the note, earnest and sad talking about not having a father and now maybe she'd have someone to give ridiculous gifts to. His wet eyes as he folded the paper and put it in his wallet. He left his people once—not for Vietnam like most of the men in his dirt town. Only sons of tobacco farmers with at least one hook for a hand don't go to war. He stayed long past intention, past broken limbs and fires his father set, past busted knees at twenty-five but after his daddy had rotted with cancer and his mama, who'd worked the fields barefoot, pulling more than any man, had said, no, she'd sell before she left it to him outright. Long past totaled cars and any hope of ease on his joints. Past gutting Baba's house in hopes of making a home for his new son who he hoped would never have to work his body 'til he was wrung through and bitter. Past fixing up the trailer. Today she wonders if they'd been better off had they stayed put, had she stayed put, but no, love, no—end stage alcoholism is a hitchhiker, and he'd have come whether you kept on taking care of him or not. On a deep inhale, she reads the text, *he's dead.*

XLIII.

There is news along the Ohio River: your time here is growing short. The landlords intend to sell and you no longer speak to the people who brought you. When people ask what happened, now you have to ask if they're referring to your marriage, or the friends you've lost, or your father-in-law who died his inevitable whiskey death—the opposite of romance, faceup in filth of his own making. And yes, you know it's time to go back to Carolina when your hands shake walking past the record store and you wish you could catch the mural whale's jet pack and fly, fly.

XLIX.

There is news along the Ohio River: she walks today with some effort to convince herself this might not be the last walk. She could have time in between last lunches and packing tape, between loading a big ass pickup full of plants she started before she knew she was leaving again. Before the realization that she would not be moving back in with her husband. Before everything but the yellow rose and the bamboo fried in the bed, eastbound and down, toward Carolina. She did not know how to say goodbye to the river, so she gathered trash along her route, a nod to mother. The sun freckling her shoulders, she walked farther than she should have, so far old injuries started gnawing at her hip where so much is stored like stones in jars she keeps for no reason. A traveler, maybe houseless, stands in the splash park soaping up, his cargo shorts drooping from the weight of water and she follows his lead, removing her headphones and shoes, peeling off socks to reveal a ridiculous tan line. She walks under the whirlybirds spinning, finds a spot next to two cackling siblings running in circles and stands still, holding herself, grateful.

L.

There is news along the Ohio River: it's your last day in Kentuckiana and your birthday to boot. Forty-five. Every birthday you are reminded that you are not a mother, but you nurture, too. All your books are packed up and you have to turn sideways to get down the shotgun long hallway. The husband from whom you've been separated for twenty-one months comes to help haul the cats and the few things remaining. Some original art, your grandpa's cowboy hat, your grandmother's tomato pin cushion. Things only you value. You have planned this farewell with a degree of ceremony because you have been bad at ritualizing transitions in the past. You are on your way out of limbo though you don't know it yet, but this country being this country, another school shooting happens the same day and the babies, the babies. But all this time, the river has kept you tethered to this earth and you will celebrate being alive tonight by seeing your first and last show at the Paristown Hall where Valerie June will introduce a cover talking about *hard times is always hanging around, but we got to call joy into being,* and then she'll sing a cover of *What A Wonderful World* and you will let it all go to a song that has always felt like a loosening of twine around your wounds.

ACKNOWLEDGMENTS

Versions of these pieces appeared in *Heavy Feather Review, The Cincinnati Review, Miracle Monocle, About Place Journal, Five South, Craft, Pithead Chapel,* and *The Cleaver.* A huge thank you to Han and Amorak of River River Books for believing in this book and being its champion. I didn't think anyone would want my odd little bird. I would also like to thank those who've continued to support me through the liminal spaces my brain & body sometimes occupies. Ben, how we survived the last decade is beyond me but I'm forever grateful we're both still here, having mostly emerged from deep shadow by doing the difficult work on ourselves the past few years. We still don't have much figured out, but I know we've got each other's back, whatever comes, whether darkness or light, in this world and the next. Erica, thank you for being who you are and encouraging me to do the same. I don't know how I would've survived our youth without you. Angela, for twenty-four years, we've laughed and cried and eaten well. Though I hated that office job all those years ago, I'm forever grateful we walked through the door on the same day. Kim, my Gemini bestie, that we only met in midlife seems like a total rip-off, but I'm grateful for our validating, grounding, and darkly comedic friendship. Jeff, Rob, Mike, and Dina, seeing you every year, though too seldom, is an anchor—it always reminds me to keep going, to keep writing, to keep putting my whole heart out there, to feel it break and heal and welcome and notice every little feeling that rises, so thank you. Violeta, I will forever be grateful that we've finally reconnected after that fateful residency in the way back. Thank you also to friends: Chloe Clark, Heather Bell-Adams, Kathy Fish (this book got its start during one of your flash weekends), Kris Bernard, Troy Palmer, Tabitha Blankenbiller, Matthew Humphrey, Hillary Leftwich, Nancy Stohlman, Jayne Martin, Marsha Timblin, Steph Post, Abigail Kemske, Sherrie Flick, Sheila Squillante, Susan Boser, David Brady, and Julie Brooks Barbour. Thank you also to Louisville for all you taught me.

BETH GILSTRAP (she/her) is a writer from Charlotte, North Carolina who likes to play with genre lines. She is the author of two story collections including *Deadheading & Other Stories* (2021), winner of the Red Hen Press Women's Prose Prize, and *I Am Barbarella: Stories* (2015) from Twelve Winters Press. She is also the author of the chapbook *No Man's Wild Laura* (2016) from Hyacinth Girl Press & EIC/publisher of the goth/punk zine, *Black Lily*. Her essays, stories, and hybrids have appeared in *Poets & Writers, Wigleaf, Craft, Bending Genres,* and *The Cincinnati Review*, among others. She and her house full of critters currently call the Charleston-metro area home. As a neurodivergent human who lives with c-PTSD, she is quite vocal about ending the stigma surrounding mental illness.

RIVER RIVER BOOKS was founded by Amorak Huey and Han VanderHart in March 2022. Inspired by the idea that you cannot step in the same river twice, two poetry editors join together to publish (at least) two exceptional poetry titles a year, as well as the Plainwater Nonfiction Series.

Poetry Catalog

An Eye in Each Square, Lauren Camp, 2023
Bullet Points: A Lyric, Jennifer A Sutherland, 2023
Dear Memphis, Rachel Edelman, 2024
A Geography That Does Not Hurt Us, Carla Sofia Ferreira, 2024
Pastoral, 1994, Joe Wilkins 2025
Your Mother's Bear Gun, Corrie Williamson, 2025
Field Notes, E.G. Cunningham, 2025
Encounters for the Living and the Dead, Jameela F. Dallis, 2025
Antibody, Elane Kim, 2026
House of Myth and Necessity, Jennifer A Sutherland, 2026
Scythe, Elizabeth Sylvia, 2026
Fifty Mothers, Preeti Vangani, 2026
The Visible Field, Zoë Ryder White, 2026
Snails of the Apocalypse, Martha Zweig, 2026
Little Automata of the Deciduous Forest, Mirande Bissell, 2027
Turn a Girl to Salt, Janet McAdams, 2027
Whale Garden, Carolyn Oliver, 2027

Plainwater Nonfiction Series

There Is News Along the Ohio River, Beth Gilstrap, 2026
Backyard Alchemy, J.D. Ho, 2026